WORLD'S
STRANGEST
BASEBALL
STORIES

by Bart Rockwell

Watermill Press

Metric Equivalents

1 inch = 2.540 centimeters

1 foot = 0.305 meters

1 mile = 1.609 kilometers

To future baseball stars
Matty J. and Marty

Cover illustration by Paulette Bogan.

LIBRARY OF CONGRESS CATALOGING-IN-PUBLICATION DATA
Rockwell, Bart, (date)
    The world's strangest baseball stories / by Bart Rockwell.
        p.   cm.
    Summary: Relates unusual stories and facts from the history of baseball.
    ISBN 0-8167-2933-6 (lib. bdg.)   ISBN 0-8167-2850-X (pbk.)
    1. Baseball—United States—Anecdotes—Juvenile literature.
    2. Baseball—United States—History—Juvenile literature.
    [1. Baseball—Miscellanea.   2. Baseball—History.]   I. Title.
    GV867.5.R63   1993
    796.357'0973—dc20   92-10120

GOING, GOING, GONE FOREVER!

Hoyt Wilhelm was a rookie pitcher for the New York Giants in 1952. In his very first major-league at bat, Hoyt smashed a home run! That's a great batting start for a young pitcher, but Hoyt's luck didn't last long. In fact, it vanished forever. Hoyt Wilhelm played 21 more years in the majors for nine different teams and appeared in 1,070 games without ever hitting another home run!

JUST FOR LUCK!

New York Yankee slugger Babe Ruth was one of the greatest home-run hitters of all time. He was also very superstitious. Babe always touched second base on his way in from the outfield, just for luck!

TEAMMATE TROUBLE

P itcher Jim Abbott of the American League's California Angels loves to meet up with old teammates during the baseball season. On July 23, 1991, Abbott outdueled Baltimore hurler Ben McDonald — a former teammate on America's Olympic baseball team — to notch a 5–4 victory and end a personal two-game losing streak. Four days later, at Yankee Stadium, Abbott faced another old pal — Yankee pitcher Scott Kamieniecki. Kamieniecki was Abbott's roommate in college at the University of Michigan. Jim renewed his old friendship with Scott by beating him 8–4!

THANKS, BRO!

B rothers Phil and Joe Niekro combined for over 500 pitching victories during their major-league careers. Both brothers were famous for throwing the knuckleball, but not for hitting the ball. In fact, Joe Niekro played in more than 300 games before he hit his first major-league home run. Joe's historic round-tripper came on May 29, 1976, when Joe's Houston Astro squad took on the Atlanta Braves. Who was the Braves' hurler who served up the meatball that Joe blasted out of the park? It was none other than his own brother, Phil!

A GOOD OUT

During a 1949 game, pitcher Ewell Blackwell of the Cincinnati Reds had the good fortune to strike out St. Louis Cardinals' all-star Stan Musial. Unfortunately, the third strike got away from catcher Dixie Howell, and Musial ended up running all the way to second base. "That guy Musial is so good," groaned Reds' manager Bucky Walters, "that even when he fans, a team is lucky to hold him to two bases!"

LETTER IMPERFECT

Baseball players Ed Als and Ken Germano never got a chance to try out for a major-league baseball team. Who was to blame? No one can be sure, but it could have been the U.S. Postal Service! In August 1991 an undelivered letter was finally returned to Manhattan College in New York City — 19 years after it was mailed! An official in the college's athletic department had mailed the letter on August 19, 1972, to Al Harper, a scout for the Boston Red Sox. The letter was a request for Harper to check out catcher Germano and outfielder Als in an upcoming All-Star game. Unfortunately, Harper never got the letter, and Ed Als and Ken Germano never got a chance for a major-league tryout.

TRADE PARADE

Pro sports teams sometimes make the stupidest trades, and baseball is no exception. The Boston Red Sox sold pitcher Babe Ruth to the New York Yankees to help pay off the mortgage on Fenway Park. The Babe later drew enough fans to his games to help build Yankee Stadium. Another dumb swap was a Canton, Ohio team's trade of future Hall of Fame pitcher Cy Young to Cleveland for a mere suit of clothes. First baseman Jack Fenton was dealt from San Francisco to a team in Memphis for a box of prunes. And poor Chattanooga shortstop Johnny Jones got his feathers ruffled when he was told to fly the coop. Jones was traded to a Charlotte, North Carolina team for a Thanksgiving turkey!

KNIGHT BASEBALL

The first baseball game in Berlin, Germany was played on June 12, 1912. To call the game, the home-plate umpire wore a suit of armor!

VICTORY WAS NO ACCIDENT

O akland A's pitcher Mike Norris took a crash course in safety while driving to the ballpark in April 1983. The brakes of Norris's BMW failed as he went down a hill, and he crashed into a pole, totalling the car. Luckily, Norris was unhurt, and he arrived at the stadium in time to pitch his team to a 5–3 victory over the Cleveland Indians.

YOUNGEST PLAYERS

T he youngest player ever to appear in a major-league game in the modern era was pitcher Joe Nuxhall, who played one game for the Cincinnati Reds in June 1944 at the age of 15 years, 314 days. He then left the majors and didn't return until 1952.

The youngest to play in the minor leagues was Joe Reliford, who played in a game for the Fitzgerald Pioneers in the Georgia State League in 1952 at the age of only 12 years, 234 days!

HOMEBODY!

H all of Famer Ty Cobb holds the major-league record for the most career steals of home. Cobb burglarized the plate a grand total of 35 times!

THE FEMININE TOUCH

The 1989 Little League World Series definitely had a feminine touch. That was the year Betty Speziale became the first female umpire to ever officiate a Little League World Series game. It was also the year that Victoria Brucker, a member of the San Pedro, California team, became the first girl to play on an American team in the Little League World Series.

ALL FOR NAUGHT

The longest shutout game in major-league history was played on April 15, 1968, when the Houston Astros beat the New York Mets 1–0 in 24 innings! On August 23, 1989, the Montreal Expos and the L.A. Dodgers came close to tying the record, when the Dodgers nipped the Expos 1–0 in 22 innings.

GOING BATTY

After striking out with the bases loaded one day, New York Yankee catcher Yogi Berra walked back to the dugout in disgust and tossed his bat away. "That bat ain't got no wood in it!" Yogi remarked.

FIRST PITCH BOO-BOO

Pitcher Jim Bibby of the Pittsburgh Pirates goofed on his very first pitch in a game against the Atlanta Braves on May 19, 1981, serving up a leadoff single to the first Braves' batter he faced. But Bibby quickly got his act together. Jim retired the next 27 batters in a row to record a one-hit, 5–0 victory over Atlanta.

OUCH! THAT SMARTS!

R on Hunt of the Montreal Expos set a major-league record in 1971, but it was a painful one. Hunt got his name in the record book by getting hit by pitched balls 50 times that season!

ONE-GAME STAR

T here's an old saying that every dog has his day. Apparently every baseball player does, too. Shortstop Cesar Gutierrez was known as a weak hitter in the major leagues, posting a lowly .235 lifetime batting average. But on June 21, 1970, Gutierrez tied a major-league record by getting seven consecutive hits (six singles, one double) in one game!

WHO'S ON FIRST?

H erb Washington of the Oakland A's stole 29 bases in 1974. There's nothing unusual about that unless you consider this: Washington stole those bases without ever coming to bat that season! Washington was the A's designated runner and never got a chance to hit.

PLEASE TRADE ME

M any professional athletes who get traded end up unhappy with the trade. But that wasn't the case with infielder Eddie Stanky. Stanky was traded three times during a five-year period in the late 1940's and early 1950's, and each time ended up on a team that went to the World Series. Eddie played for the Brooklyn Dodgers in 1947, the Boston Braves in 1948, and the New York Giants in 1951. Unfortunately, Stanky's luck ran out when his teams reached the championship. They were all losers in the World Series!

ONE-GAME WHIZ

O n May 6, 1953, rookie pitcher Alva "Bobo" Holloman of the St. Louis Browns did something that no other major-league pitcher has ever duplicated: He threw a no-hitter in his very first major-league game. Unfortunately for Bobo, he never pitched as well again, and was soon farmed out to the minors. He never returned to pitch in the major leagues!

LEFT, RIGHT! LEFT, RIGHT!

Y ou've heard of switch-hitters. But have you ever heard of switch-pitchers? Four ambidextrous pitchers played in the major leagues in the early days of the game. As batters came to the plate, the pitchers would switch from pitching with one arm to the other. The tricky pitchers were Tony Mullane, who played for the Louisville Eclipse in 1882, Larry Corcoran, who played for the Chicago White Stockings in 1884, John Roach, who pitched for the New York Giants in 1887, and Elton "Icebox" Chamberlain, who played for the Louisville Eclipse in 1888. Chamberlain was the only switch-pitcher to ever win a major-league game in which he switch pitched. In 1969 the major leagues outlawed switch-pitching.

M arv Throneberry was a first baseman for the New York Mets in 1962 and had a reputation for making lots of errors. Sometimes it seemed like Marv just couldn't hold on to the ball. On his birthday that year, Mets' player Richie Ashburn walked over to congratulate him. "We were going to give you a cake, Marv," said Ashburn, "but we thought you'd drop it!"

UP, UP AND AWAY!

O akland A's slugger Dave Kingman probably blasted the most bizarre double in baseball history on May 4, 1984 at the Hubert H. Humphrey Metrodome in Minneapolis. Kingman smashed a pop-up that sailed toward the roof of the indoor stadium just behind the pitcher's mound. The ball hit a drainage hole in the bottom layer of the Metrodome's fabric ceiling and vanished. It never came down! Umpire Jim Evans had no choice but to award Kingman a ground-rule double on his bizarre shot to the ceiling!

HOMER HEX!

Walter Maranille of the Pittsburgh Pirates set a dubious National League home-run record in 1922. Maranille went to the plate 672 times that season without hitting a single home run.

Doc Cramer of Boston set the American League homer hex record in 1938. Doc went to the plate a record 658 times that season without belting a single round-tripper!

POWERFUL PITCHER

Pitchers are supposed to be good at throwing the ball, not hitting it. Apparently, hurler Wes Ferrell didn't know that. Ferrell holds the major-league record for the most lifetime homers by a pitcher. Wes smashed 38 four-sackers in his career and belted 9 over the fence in a single season in 1931.

STRIKEOUT KING

Reggie Jackson is best known as one of the greatest home-run hitters of all time. But sometimes even a great slugger misses his mark. Reggie whiffed 2,597 times in his 9,864 career at-bats, more than any other major-league player in history.

WHOOSH

ABSENT ALL-STAR

Mike Schmidt, a slugging third baseman for the Philadelphia Phillies, was voted to the All-Star team a number of times during his career. However, in 1989 Schmidt was nearing the end of his illustrious career and decided to call it quits. Mike announced his retirement in May 1989. Even though Schmidt was retired and technically ineligible to play in the All-Star Game that season, baseball fans around the country voted Mike Schmidt the starting third baseman of the National League squad for the July All-Star contest. It was the first time in baseball history that an inactive player was ever voted a starting role in an All-Star Game. Mike attended the game, of course, but he didn't play.

A LONG WALK

Boston Red Sox slugger Jimmy Foxx walked six times in a row in a single game on June 16, 1938, still the record for a nine-inning game.

WHAT'S IN A NAME?

When he was born, his father named him after Hall of Fame baseball catcher Mickey Cochrane. The lad ended up following in his namesake's footsteps— he became a major-league baseball player, and was later elected to the Hall of Fame. His name was Mickey Mantle!

LITTLE BIG LEAGUER

The first Little League player to ever make it to baseball's major leagues was pitcher Joey Jay. Jay made the roster of the Milwaukee Braves in 1953 and went on to win 99 major-league games.

OH, BROTHER!

In a game in 1963, the San Francisco Giants had an interesting outfield trio. The last names of the left fielder, center fielder, and right fielder were all Alou. The Alou brothers—Felipe, Matty, and Jesus— all played together in the same outfield that day!

TWO FOR ONE

The Framingham (Mass.) State College baseball team came up with an interesting but illegal way to shorten those sometimes long and boring double-headers. Framingham's coach came up with a winner-take-all deal for games against Salem State and Boston State on May 4 and May 6, 1980. The deal was simple. The team that won the first game of the doubleheader also got credit for winning the second game, which was never actually played! Statistics for the first game were real while stats for the second game were made up.

When the two-for-one deal was finally exposed, Framingham went back to the traditional way of playing doubleheaders...after a few coaching resignations.

PHILADELPHIA STORY

To win baseball's Triple Crown, a player has to lead his league in home runs, batting average, and runs batted in. It's a very difficult task, and very few players have ever accomplished it. Strange then, that in 1933 there were Triple Crown winners in both leagues. What makes the 1933 "double Triple" even more astounding is the fact that both winners played in the same city. Chuck Klein of the Philadelphia Phillies won the National League Triple Crown (.368 BA, 28 HR's, and 120 RBI's), and Jimmy Foxx of the Philadelphia A's won the American League Triple Crown (.356 BA, 48 HR's, and 163 RBI's). It sure was a good year to play in Philadelphia!

SHORT STORY

In 1967 Central High School in Minneapolis had a pinch hitter named Ricky Raski who never failed to get on base. Ricky reached base safely every time he batted, but never got a single hit. The reason? Ricky Raski was only 3' 3" tall. No matter how hard the pitchers tried, they couldn't master his small strike zone. Ricky Raski walked every time he batted that season!

QUIET PLEASE!

In August 1981 Angel Rodriguez, a catcher for the Alexandria team of the Carolina League, got in trouble for talking too much behind the plate. Rodriguez was caught telling opposing Latin American batters what pitch was being thrown before it was delivered to the plate. Rodriguez tipped off certain batters by speaking Spanish. Unfortunately for Angel, he was caught and suspended from baseball for four years.

CLOSE BUT NO PRIZE

Jimmy Dykes was a big-league manager for a long time. In fact, Dykes managed in the American and National Leagues for 21 years. Unfortunately for Jimmy, the only record he ever set is best left forgotten. Dykes has the dubious distinction of being the man who managed the longest in the majors without ever winning a pennant.

PITCHER'S NIGHTMARE

Every pitcher dreams of hurling a no-hitter. On July 1, 1990, pitcher Andy Hawkins of the New York Yankees had his dream come true. Unfortunately, it turned into a nightmare. Hawkins no-hit the Chicago White Sox for nine innings, but ended up the victim of the most lopsided regulation no-hit defeat in history when the Sox beat the Yanks 4–0. Chicago scored all its runs on errors and walks in the eighth inning of the game.

WHAT CLOUT!

Almost every baseball fan knows that Roger Maris of the New York Yankees set a record by smashing 61 home runs in a single season. The 1980 New York Mets didn't quite have a home-run hitter of Maris' caliber. In fact, in 1980 the entire Mets squad accounted for only 61 home runs—the same number Maris hit all by himself in his record-breaking year.

FROM GOOD TO BAD

Pat Seerey of the Chicago White Sox had a real roller-coaster ride in July 1948. Seerey tied a major-league record by belting four home runs in one game on July 18. The very next week he set another major-league record by striking out seven times in a doubleheader on July 24.

PASS THE BUCK

A sportswriter once asked Yankee catcher Yogi Berra what he'd do if he found a million dollars. Yogi answered, "Well, if the guy who lost it was real poor, I'd give it back to him."

BIG HITTERS

Talk about slugging teammates! When they played together for the New York Yankees, Babe Ruth and Lou Gehrig combined for a total of 859 home runs, the highest ever combined home-run total for two teammates. Hank Aaron and Eddie Matthews of the Milwaukee and Atlanta Braves combined for 857 homers during the years they played together.

UNDERHANDED TRICK

Carl Mays of the New York Yankees had a very unusual delivery for a major-league baseball pitcher. Mays, who starred in the majors during the 1920's, threw the ball underhanded. His unorthodox style was very successful. In 1920 Carl won 26 games, and in 1921 he notched 27 wins. In all, under-handed hurler Carl Mays won more than 200 games during his career.

HE'S EVERYWHERE!

Shortstop Jose Oquendo of the St. Louis Cardinals was a busy ball player during the 1988 season. That year Oquendo became the first National League performer in over 70 years to play all nine positions in a single season! The last National League player to accomplish that feat was Gene Paulette, also of the Cards, who played all nine positions in 1918.

Cesar Tovar of the American League's Minnesota Twins, however, topped the performances of Oquendo and Paulette. Tovar played all nine positions *in a single game* in 1968! Bert Campaneris of the Kansas City Athletics once did the same thing as a promotional gimmick in 1965.

PLAYER SALARY

The Detroit Tigers once settled their spring-training bill with an Augusta, Georgia team by leaving one of their players, Ed Cicohe, with the Augusta team as payment!

SHORTSTOP STRESS?

Is baseball good for your health? According to a study done by the Metropolitan Life Insurance Company, ball players enjoy longer life spans than males in the general population. The study also reported that, of all players, third basemen live the longest. Shortstops have the shortest life span!

HOW DID THEY MANAGE THAT?

In 1960 Cleveland Indians general manager Frank Lane worked out an unusual trade with Detroit Tigers general manager Bill DeWitt. The Indians, who were in fourth place in the league, needed a change. The Tigers, who were in sixth place, also needed a change. But instead of swapping players, the two teams traded managers. Manager Joe Gordon of the Indians was sent to Detroit in exchange for Tigers manager Jimmy Dykes. Unfortunately, the trade didn't help much—the Indians finished fourth, while the Tigers stayed in sixth place.

HE NEVER GOT RUSTY

Joseph Jerome McGinnity became famous as a baseball "Iron Man" in 1903 while pitching for the old New York Giants. McGinnity was a tireless hurler who pitched both games of a doubleheader on five different occasions in 1903. "Iron Man" McGinnity won three of those five doubleheaders (a total of six victories) and had split decisions in the other two.

HOT AND COLD

Talk about wacky weather. On July 4, 1933, a baseball game in Gallup, New Mexico had to be delayed because of searing hot weather. Two hours later, after play had been resumed, the same game had to be called off because of a raging snowstorm!

LUCKY SIX

In 1902 Tommy Leach of the Pittsburgh Pirates won the National League home-run crown. But it wasn't really much of an achievement. Leach topped all home-run hitters in the league with a measly six round-trippers.

WHAT A STEAL!

Josh Devore of the old New York Giants put on quite a base-stealing show in 1912. He stole a record four bases in a single inning while making two trips to the plate!

LITTLE BIG PROBLEM

In 1979 three fourth-grade baseball teams in Oklahoma had a heated dispute over a Little League game. In the contest, the Patrick Henry Giants beat the Marshall Hawks on a last-inning, two-out home run. The Hawks protested that the Giants used an illegal substitute. The Giants ended up forfeiting the game, which upset the McClure Cardinals, another team. McClure protested because the Hawks' win affected their place in the league standings. The disagreement became so intense that the teams ended up going to civil court to settle the matter! A judge finally ruled that the Hawks and Giants were to be considered division co-champions, and that in the league playoff the Giants should be seeded first and McClure second. The judgment satisfied everyone involved.

NAME GAME

How can two players appear in the same baseball box score on the same side when one is traded for the other? Here's how it happened in August 1979. Ray Burris of the Chicago Cubs played in a game against the Cincinnati Reds on May 10, 1979 that was suspended before the game was finished. Burris was later involved in a trade that brought pitcher Dick Tidrow to the Cubs. When the suspended game was finished later that season, Tidrow pitched in it. The result was that Ray Burris and Dick Tidrow appeared in the same box score on the same side, even though they'd been traded for each other!

GOING, GOING, YOU'RE GONE!

On August 15, 1982, Joel Youngblood of the New York Mets smacked a two-run single against the Chicago Cubs. When he returned to the Mets dugout, he received congratulations and some shocking news. He'd been traded to the Montreal Expos during the middle of the game! After the game, Youngblood flew to Philadelphia to join his new Expo teammates in a night game against the Phillies. He got a hit in the game, thus becoming the only player to get a hit for two different teams in two different cities on the same day!

MARATHON MAN

Experts estimate that Hall of Famer Ty Cobb ran a total of 99 miles as a base runner during his career.

PHEW!

HAT TRICK

B aseball great Eddie Collins had an unusual superstition. He always carried a wad of chewing gum on the bottom of his cap. Whenever he was at bat and got two strikes on him, he'd pluck the gum off of his hat and chew it vigorously for good luck.

SHOW ME THE WAY TO GO HOME

O n September 21, 1956, the powerful New York Yankees took on their archrivals, the Boston Red Sox. The Yankee sluggers had no trouble getting men on base, but they had lots of difficulty driving runners home! In fact, they left 20 runners stranded on the base paths that day — a major-league record that stands to this day!

A HOMER-LESS MAN

I nfielder Tommy Thevenow, who began playing in the National League in 1924, hit two homers during the 1926 season. After that he went to bat a total of 3,347 times for the rest of his major-league career — without ever hitting another round-tripper. And that is a baseball record!

WHAT A START!

R ookie William Duggleby of the old Philadelphia Phillies made quite an impression in his first major-league at bat. Duggleby stepped to the plate with the bases loaded and smacked a grand-slam home run on April 21, 1898. No other player has ever hit a grand slam in his first major-league at bat!

SWAP MEET

O ne of the wackiest trades in baseball history took place during a doubleheader between the Chicago Cubs and the St. Louis Cardinals on May 22, 1922. Max Flack of the Cubs was traded for Cliff Heathcote of the Cardinals at the end of the first game. Before the start of the second game of the doubleheader, the two players swapped uniforms and switched sides!

HELLO! GOOD-BYE!

A manager getting thrown out of a game by an umpire is nothing new to baseball. However, San Diego Padres manager Steve Boros came up with a new twist to the old story in 1986. Boros got kicked out of a game before it even started! Here's what happened.

The night before, the Padres had played the Atlanta Braves. In that contest the Braves pulled off an astonishing triple play. When Padres player Steve Garvey, usually a mild-mannered gentleman, protested the call, umpire Charlie Williams threw Garvey out of the game. It was the first time in Garvey's career that he'd been given the gate by an umpire. Manager Boros protested in Garvey's behalf, but to no avail.

Before the Braves-Padres game the next day, Boros walked up to umpire Williams with a video-tape of the triple play, as proof that Williams blew the call the day before. Williams didn't want to see the tape—or Steve Boros. He tossed the Padres' manager out of the game before it even started!

WARTIME WONDERS

D uring World War II the armed forces drafted and enlisted most of the best players from both baseball leagues. To fill out their rosters, teams in the American and National Leagues used some players who were physically unable to serve in the war effort.

Two of the most inspiring players in major-league baseball during those wartime years were Bert Shepard and Pete Gray. Shepard, who played occasionally for the Washington Senators, had only one leg. Gray, who played in 77 games for the St. Louis Browns, had only one arm.

THE OLD COLLEGE TRY

T he first college baseball game in history was played between Amherst College and Williams College on July 1, 1859. It wasn't exactly a close game. Amherst won 66–32!

OUT OF LUCK

P itcher Steve Carlton of the St. Louis Cardinals had good luck and bad luck in a game against the New York Mets on September 15, 1969. Carlton had the good fortune to strike out a then-record 19 Mets in that contest. Steve also had the misfortune to lose the game 4–3, on a home run by Mets outfielder Ron Swoboda.

THE MISTY METS

T alk about a player being in a fog. In 1979, a game between the New York Mets and the Pittsburgh Pirates was officially fogged out. When the game began at twilight that evening, the skies in New York were clear enough. As the contest wore on, however, a weird mist rolled into Shea Stadium and settled on the playing field. The overhead lights took on an eerie glow as the thick fog made it almost impossible to see. The fog was so bad that a routine pop-up to center field became a triple because the outfielders never saw the ball. The umpires temporarily halted play, hoping the fog would clear. It didn't. At 2:15 A.M., the umpires decided to suspend play and allow the teams to finish the game another day when the weather was more cooperative. It was the first time a major-league baseball game had ever been fogged out!

WHOOPS!

Shortstop Roger Peckinpaugh of the Washington Senators was voted the Most Valuable Player in the American League in 1925. However, his performance in the 1925 World Series wasn't very valuable. Peckinpaugh committed a record eight errors in the Series against Pittsburgh, which helped the Pirates take the world title.

I NEVER MISS!

With so many pitches thrown to them in each game, catchers are bound to make errors. But Yogi Berra was a steady man behind the plate. From 1957 to 1959, Yogi caught 148 games without committing a single error, still a major-league record.

NO SUBS PLEASE

Connie Mack's Philadelphia Athletics played through two of the five World Series they won without ever using a substitution of any kind. The Athletics didn't use a relief pitcher, a pinch hitter, or even a pinch runner.

NOT A BIG HIT!

Major-league baseball pitchers are not expected to hit the ball, and the following pitchers obviously knew it. Pitcher Ron Herbel played major-league baseball from 1963 to 1971 and posted a measly .029 career batting average. Hurler Jim Duckworth didn't do much better. Playing from 1963 to 1966, his career average was only .034. However, even Herbel and Duckworth topped the average posted by Houston Astro pitcher Fred Gladding. Gladding, who played from 1961 to 1973, got only one hit in 65 at bats, for a career average of .016!

HOT TOPIC

In the old days of baseball, teams often got into fights. In a game between the Boston Red Sox and the Baltimore Orioles in May 1894, a fight really got out of hand. As the players on the field started to fight, so did the fans in the stands. A riot was soon in progress at the ballpark. During the scuffle, the wooden stands accidentally caught fire. The fire spread so fast that the ballpark and 170 other buildings near it all burned down. It just goes to prove that when your temper gets hot the best thing you can do is cool down!

ZEROS

H ow can an entire major-league team have every player on its roster enter a game and then finish it with exactly the same batting averages they started with? It sounds impossible, but it happened on April 6, 1940, when the Chicago White Sox met the Cleveland Indians on Opening Day. Since it was Opening Day, the Chicago players all entered the game with a .000 average. On that day Bob Feller of the Indians opened the season by hurling a no-hitter against the White Sox. So when the game was over, every Chicago player still had a .000 average.

A LITTLE TRAVELING MUSIC

P itcher Bob Miller really got around. From 1957 to 1974 Miller played on ten different major-league teams. He played for the St. Louis Cardinals, the New York Mets (twice), the Los Angeles Dodgers, the Minnesota Twins, the Cleveland Indians, the Chicago White Sox, the Chicago Cubs, the San Diego Padres (twice), the Pittsburgh Pirates, and the Detroit Tigers. And just to top things off, he began his coaching career with yet another team, the Toronto Blue Jays!

BEGIN AGAIN

B ecause major-league baseball players are traded to various teams, they sometimes do a lot of traveling. Oddly enough, four of baseball's greatest home-run hitters started their careers with one team in a city, and then ended their careers in that same city with another team. Babe Ruth started his major-league career with the Boston Red Sox and ended it with the Boston Braves. Willie Mays began his career with the New York Giants and finished with the New York Mets. Jimmy Foxx started his playing days with the Philadelphia A's and ended up with the Philadelphia Phillies. Hank Aaron, the greatest home-run hitter of them all, started his career with the Milwaukee Braves and was a member of the Milwaukee Brewers when he hung up his spikes.

OLD PRO

S ome baseball players, like fine wine, improve with age. Catcher Carlton Fisk of the Chicago White Sox proved that on July 9, 1991 at the annual All-Star Game. Fisk, who was 43 years and 6 months old at the time, singled in the game to become the oldest player ever to get a hit in an All-Star Game. Before Fisk, Ted Williams was the oldest player to enjoy that distinction. Williams was 41 years and 10 months old when he singled in the 1961 All-Star contest.

IT TAKES A THIEF

Maury Wills of the Los Angeles Dodgers is one of the greatest base thieves in baseball history. Maury set a record by stealing 104 bases in a single season in 1962. For having such a great year, Wills was awarded the jeweled Hickock Belt as the nation's outstanding pro athlete. Over the years, Wills worried that the belt, valued at $50,000, might be stolen from his house, so he presented it to a Las Vegas club for safekeeping. In July 1981, someone broke into the club and stole the belt Maury Wills had won for stealing bases!

TRIPLE TROUBLE

Wacky Babe Herman of the old Brooklyn Dodgers once turned a bases-loaded triple into a double play! Herman hit a long ball, but in his zeal to reach third base, passed two of his fellow runners on the base paths. The runners Babe passed were thereby called out.

A WAVE GOOD-BYE

Sometimes pitchers get sent to the showers when they pitch poorly. Hurler Henry Heitman got sent to the showers—and ended up on the ocean! On July 27, 1918 Heitman was the starting pitcher for the Brooklyn Dodgers against the St. Louis Cardinals. The first four batters Heitman faced all got hits. Henry was yanked out of the game. But he didn't stop in the locker room. Heitman packed his stuff, left the stadium, and enlisted in the Navy! Henry Heitman never played major-league baseball again.

GOING ON STRIKE

In 1987 Rob Deer of the Milwaukee Brewers set an American League record by striking out 186 times in 134 games, almost 1 1/2 strikeouts per game!

BLASTED!

In 1930, over the course of two games, the great home-run hitter Babe Ruth hit five round-trippers in six official visits to the plate!

PHEW!

In 1906 the New York Yankees played ten baseball games in just five days. The team played five consecutive doubleheaders, meeting the Washington Senators for six of those games and the Philadelphia Athletics and the Boston Red Sox for two games each.

DEAD DUCK

In 1974 slugger Willie Horton of the Detroit Tigers swung hard at a pitch and "fowled" it high into the air. The ball went up, and seconds later a dead pigeon dropped onto the field near home plate. Horton's foul ball had accidentally hit and killed it!

THAT'S A SHAME

A lot of baseball players have gotten into the record book by hitting three home runs in a single game. However, hitting three home runs in an entire season isn't much to be proud of—especially if three homers is all your *entire team* hits in a season. Nevertheless, the Chicago White Sox of the American League set a record in 1908 for hitting the fewest home runs in a season. The entire team hit a total of only three round-trippers.

FAMILY AFFAIR

Sandy and Roberto Alomar made the 1991 baseball All-Star Game a family affair. The Alomar brothers were both voted to the American League All-Star squad. Sandy's election marked the first time a rookie catcher was ever named to the starting team. It was also the first time brothers were elected to the squad since All-Star balloting was returned to the fans in 1970, which ironically, was the same year that the boys' father, Sandy Alomar, Sr., was a member of the AL All-Star squad. The Alomars joined Dom, Vince, and Joe DiMaggio as the only baseball families to ever have three members named to the All-Star team.

HEADS UP!

Manager Greg Riddoch of the San Diego Padres suffered a bizarre injury in 1991. Riddoch received a mild concussion on July 3, 1991, when Benito Santiago, a Padres player, grounded out and threw his batting helmet in disgust. The helmet inadvertently hit Manager Riddoch on the head!

IN REVERSE

Outfielder Jimmy Piersall, one of baseball's wackiest players, was a member of the New York Mets when he hit his 100th major-league home run. Jimmy was so happy that he wanted to do something to make the event even more special for himself and the fans. Instead of running the bases the regular way after his clout, Jimmy turned around and circled all of the bases running backwards. Everyone loved Jimmy Piersall's wacky stunt, except the people who make the baseball rules. The next year, they made circling the bases backwards after hitting a home run illegal.

LOSING STREAK

Pitcher Cliff Curtis of the Boston Braves didn't have much luck on the mound in the early 1900's. Curtis lost 23 consecutive baseball games from June 13, 1910 to May 22, 1911.

OUT-MAKER

B rooklyn Dodger pitcher Clarence Mitchell didn't have much luck at the plate in the 1920 World Series against the Cleveland Indians. In his first time at bat, Mitchell hit into a double play. In his very next at-bat, he lined a ball to Cleveland second baseman Bill Wambsganss, who pulled off the only unassisted triple play in World Series history. In just two swings of the bat, Clarence Mitchell caused five outs!

BAD ENDING

J oe Borden of the old Boston Beaneaters was the first pitcher in baseball history to hurl a no-hitter. Joe threw his no-hitter at the beginning of the 1876 season. Unfortunately, after that historic outing Joe started to experiment with his delivery and lost his pitching touch. Borden was eventually dropped from the Beaneaters' roster, and finished the 1876 season as Boston's stadium groundskeeper.

GO HOME!

N ew York Yankee stars Lou Gehrig and Babe Ruth were best known for hitting home runs, but they were also nimble base runners. Gehrig holds the Yankee record for the most steals of home with 15. Lou's teammate, Babe Ruth, stole home ten times!

KID STUFF

When future Hall of Famer Mel Ott came up to the major leagues to play for the New York Giants, he was a young sixteen-year-old catcher. Manager John McGraw had lots of catchers but needed an outfielder. "Ever play the outfield?" he asked Ott.

Sixteen-year-old Mel Ott answered in a serious voice. "Yes, sir, when I was a kid!"

TARGET PRACTICE

First baseman Frank Chance of the Chicago Cubs was hit five times by pitched balls in a double-header on May 30, 1904. OUCH!

GO EDDIE GO!

Second baseman Eddie Collins of the Philadelphia Athletics once stole six bases in a single game. He did it against the Detroit Tigers on September 11, 1912. Then, just for good measure, Eddie again stole six bases in a single game, eleven days later against the St. Louis Browns!

A HOT TIME

On July 8, 1980, an All-Star-Game show at Dodger Stadium in Los Angeles turned out to be a really hot performance. As singer Toni Tennille belted out her rendition of the national anthem, rockets were set off in the stadium. The rockets landed in some hills behind the center-field wall and ignited a tremendous brush fire. The blaze was eventually extinguished, but smoke was still rising from the area when the game started.

ENDLESS BASEBALL

The longest professional baseball game in history took place in 1981. It was between the Pawtucket Red Sox and the Rochester Red Wings of the International League. The game began on April 19, 1981 at 8 P.M. and continued until 4:07 A.M. the following day, when the deadlocked contest was finally suspended.

The game was resumed 66 days later, and was eventually won by Pawtucket 3–2. In all, the game lasted a record 8 hours, 25 minutes—a total of 33 innings! Now that's a lot of baseball!

SCORING RACE

When the Chicago Cubs played the Philadelphia Phillies on August 25, 1922, the contest turned into a wild scoring game. The Cubs lost to the Phillies 26–23, which is a National League record for the most runs scored in one game by both teams.

BLIND LUCK

Many baseball games have been delayed because of rain, but on September 7, 1973, a twilight game between the Montreal Expos and the New York Mets had to be delayed because it was too *sunny*.

The sun setting over the top of the Expos' stadium sent glaring rays directly into the eyes of the first baseman. The bright sun was so bad that the first baseman couldn't see well enough to catch balls thrown to him. For safety, the umpires delayed the game 11 minutes so the sun could sink below the stadium's rim.

LEFT OUT

Pitcher Jerry Reuss of the Los Angeles Dodgers was tough on left-handed batters during the 1981 baseball season. In fact, Reuss only gave up one home run all season to a left-handed hitter. The player who spoiled Reuss's almost perfect performance against lefties was Joe Morgan of the Houston Astros.

NOT AGAIN!

Most fans agree that an unassisted triple play is the rarest play in the sport of baseball. However, in 1927 two unassisted triple plays occurred in only two days! The first was pulled off by shortstop Jim Cooney of the Chicago Cubs on May 30, 1927. In a game against the Pittsburgh Pirates, Cooney caught a liner hit by Paul Waner, stepped on second to retire Waner's brother, Lloyd, before he could return to the base, and then tagged out Clyde Barnhart, who was trying to run back to first base.

A day later, on May 31, first baseman Johnny Neun of the Detroit Tigers duplicated Cooney's triple-play feat. In a game against the Cleveland Indians, Neun caught a liner hit by Homer Summa, tagged out Charlie Jamieson, who was approaching from first, and then raced over to tag second to retire Glenn Myatt for out number three.

WHAT A PITCHER!

Today, if a pitcher wins 20 games, it's an outstanding feat. But in the old days of baseball, winning 20 games was good—but not great. Hurler Tim Keefe of the New York Metropolitans won 30 games or more on the mound for 7 *consecutive seasons* in the 1880's. In 1883, Keefe won 41 games and lost 26. If that wasn't astounding enough, in 1886 Tim won 42 games and lost only 20!

HANDS UP!

William "Buck" Ewing was a catcher for the old New York Giants in the 1880's. Buck had an interesting way of catching. He wore gloves on *both* hands. The glove on his throwing hand had cutouts for his fingers, so he could grip the ball to throw it.

DANDY SANDY

Sandy Koufax of the Los Angeles Dodgers was one of the greatest pitchers of all time. Koufax was the first National League pitcher to record over 300 strikeouts in a season (striking out 306 in 1963), and he topped his own record twice after that (382 in 1965 and 317 in 1966).

Strangely enough, Koufax never pitched a game until he was 15 years old. He believed his best sport was basketball, and he went to the University of Cincinnati on a basketball scholarship. Once there, he tried out for and made the baseball team as a sideline to his basketball playing. Koufax proved to be so successful as a college baseball player that he was signed to a major-league contract and finally gave up his basketball career.

TRAVELING AROUND

Frank Robinson, a Hall of Famer who played for teams in both the American and National Leagues, hit at least one home run in each of 32 different major-league stadiums during regular-season play from 1956 to 1977.

WORST TO FIRST

alk about making a comeback! In 1990 the Minnesota Twins and the Atlanta Braves both finished dead last in their divisions in the American and National Leagues. Then the teams did a complete reversal. In 1991 the Twins and Braves won pennants in their respective leagues, and then met in the 1991 World Series, which Minnesota won 4 games to 3. In a single year, each team went from last place to first!

FINDERS KEEPERS

n the early days of baseball, balls hit into the stands had to be returned to the field of play. Stadium ushers often had to pry baseballs out of the hands of fans who caught them! Ed Barrow, who managed the Boston Red Sox and was later president of the New York Yankees, began the practice of allowing fans to keep balls hit into the stands.

ANYBODY GOOD ON YOUR TEAM?

The pitching staff of the 1954 Cleveland Indians wasn't too shabby, to say the least. The roster included four pitchers who eventually won more than 200 games each during their careers. The Indian hurlers were led by Early Wynn (300 career wins), Bob Feller (266 career wins), Bob Lemon (207 career wins), and Hal Newhouser (201 career wins). Not surprisingly, the Cleveland pitching staff won an American League record 111 games in 1954.

SHAKY START

Game three of the 1989 baseball World Series between the Oakland A's and the San Francisco Giants started out with a rumble instead of a bang. The game, slated to be played at San Francisco's Candlestick Park, got off to an extremely shaky start. As the TV announcers were doing the pregame warmup, an earthquake struck, causing the stadium to vibrate and shake. There was a loss of power and the stadium lights dimmed. Luckily everyone remained calm and no one was injured.

However, Candlestick Park was damaged and the game had to be postponed. It was the first time in history that a World Series game had been "quaked" out.

CAREER GAME

Shortstop Johnny Burnett of the Cleveland Indians had a big game against the Philadelphia Athletics on July 10, 1932. The Indian infielder collected nine hits in the extra-inning game to set a major-league record.

HARRY FOR HARRY

Early in 1962 the New York Mets made a trade with the Detroit Tigers for a catcher. The catcher's name was Harry Chiti. The Mets-Tigers deal called for Detroit to send Chiti to New York in exchange for $75,000 and a player to be named later. In the fall of 1962 the Mets finally completed the deal by returning a player to Detroit. That player was none other than Harry Chiti! The Mets ended up paying $75,000 for the privilege of trading Harry Chiti for Harry Chiti!

HOW MANY STRIKES?

Hall of Famer Walter Johnson accomplished an amazing feat pitching for the Washington Senators on April 15, 1911. Johnson struck out four consecutive batters in a single inning! Four batters came to the plate that inning, because the Washington catcher dropped a third strike, allowing one hitter to reach first base safely.

WAY TO GO, BABE

When Babe Ruth smacked 60 home runs in 1927, it was quite a feat. Until then, no other *team* in major-league baseball had even come close to hitting that many round-trippers in a season!

SWITCH

Garry Templeton of the St. Louis Cardinals established a strange major-league record in 1979. Templeton became the first switch-hitter in baseball history to collect at least 100 hits batting right-handed and at least 100 hits batting left-handed. (In fact, he collected 111 hits batting left-handed!)

ACCIDENTAL HELP

Mordecai Peter Centennial Brown lost most of his right index finger in a farm accident when he was just a boy. However, that awful accident helped make Mordecai "Three-Finger" Brown a famous pitcher in the major leagues. Because he was missing a finger, Brown's pitches had a natural sinking motion that fooled batters. Mordecai spent 14 years as a major-league hurler and won 20 games or more for 6 consecutive years during the early 1900's.

WATCH THE BIRDIE

Casey Stengel was one of baseball's original pranksters. Stengel played with the old Brooklyn Dodgers until he was traded to the Pittsburgh Pirates in 1918. When Casey returned to Brooklyn as a Pirate player, he pulled one of the wackiest stunts in the history of baseball. After the stadium announcer called out Stengel's name in the lineup, he stepped out onto the field and tipped his hat to the crowd. When he did, a canary that was hidden in his cap flew out— much to the crowd's delight!

FAST GAME

T he shortest nine-inning major-league game in history took place on September 28, 1919. It took the New York Giants only 51 minutes to beat the Philadelphia Phillies 6–1.

WACKY RULES

M ajor-league baseball has had some strange rules. In 1887, for example, bases on balls were counted as hits toward a player's average, and each batter got 4 strikes instead of three every time he stepped to the plate. Both of those rules were changed the following year.

IT RUNS IN THE FAMILY

A lmost every baseball fan knows that Joe DiMaggio set a major-league record by hitting safely in an amazing 56 straight games in 1941. However, Joe's brother, Dom, wasn't too shabby a hitter either. Dom DiMaggio hit safely in 34 straight games in 1949.

LAST CHANCE

C hances for a victory looked slim for the Cleveland Indians in a game against the Washington Senators on May 23, 1901. Washington was leading 13–5. Cleveland was batting in the bottom of the ninth with 2 outs and no men on base. Then an amazing thing happened. Cleveland scored a record 9 runs in the bottom of the last inning to notch a 14–13 victory!

SPLIT DECISION

Hall of Famer "Big Ed" Delahanty was a powerful hitter. During the early days of baseball he once hit a ball so hard that it split right in half! Delahanty was also a consistent hitter. In 1899 he led the National League with a .408 batting average. In 1902 Delahanty's .376 was tops in the American League. He is the only player to win batting crowns in both leagues. One of Ed's greatest hitting feats was collecting five hits in five trips to the plate in one game in 1896. Four of those hits were home runs!

PROUD POP

In 1969 New York Met Ron Swoboda and his teammates were playing the Los Angeles Dodgers on the west coast. Back home in New York, Ron's wife, Cecilia, was about to deliver the Swoboda's first child. Of course, there is a three-hour time difference between Los Angeles and New York, so when the Swobodas' baby boy was born around 1 A.M. on Saturday in New York, it was about 10 P.M. on Friday in Los Angeles. When news of the birth reached the west coast during the game, a  special message was flashed on the scoreboard. "Congratulations, Ron Swoboda," the message read. "Your new son was born tomorrow morning."

SONG NOTES

Jack Norworth wrote the lyrics to baseball's anthem, "Take Me Out to the Ball Game" in 1906. At the time, however, Norworth had never been to a baseball game in his life, and didn't attend a game until 1940!

A MINI WAVE

Catcher Yogi Berra of the New York Yankees was never at a loss for a funny line. Once, a batter hit a pop-up down the third-base line. Berra and Yankee third baseman Clete Boyer collided trying to catch the ball, which dropped to the ground safely. Boyer looked at Yogi and shouted, "What's the matter, Yogi? Couldn't you yell for it?"

Berra just shrugged and replied, "Sure! But I thought you could hear me waving at you."

CANNED HEAT

Hall of Famer Rogers Hornsby found playing on a baseball team much easier than managing one. After his playing days were over, Hornsby was hired to manage the Chicago Cubs by team owner Bill Veeck, Sr. Unfortunately, he didn't do a very good job and was fired by Veeck, Sr. in 1932.

Twenty years later, Hornsby was hired by Veeck's son, Bill Veeck, Jr. to manage the St. Louis Browns baseball team. Again Hornsby didn't fare very well. He was fired by Bill Veeck, Jr. in 1952. Rogers Hornsby is the only Hall of Famer to be fired as a manager by both father and son team owners.

WORDS TO THE WISE

When asked what a ball player in a slump needs most, Hall of Fame manager Miller Higgins replied, "A string of good alibis."

LONG HAUL

When Ken Babbage handed Cincinnati Reds officials the baseball for opening-day ceremonies in 1980, it was the end of a long trip for Ken. Babbage had walked 430 miles from a baseball factory in St. Louis to Cincinnati to hand-deliver the new baseball.

ONCE IS ENOUGH

Pitchers Frank Wurm, Joe Cleary, Harley Grossman, and Fritz Fisher didn't exactly have illustrious major-league careers. In fact, their careers began and ended in the blink of an eye. All four hurlers pitched only one-third of an inning each in their major-league careers. Wurm retired one batter as a member of the Brooklyn Dodgers in 1944. Cleary of the Washington Senators got out one batter in 1945. Grossman of the Washington Senators retired one batter in 1952, and Fisher got out only a single foe while playing for the Detroit Tigers in 1964.

LIKE FATHER LIKE SON

In 1990 Ken Griffey, Sr. and Ken Griffey, Jr. were both members of the Seattle Mariners. While the Griffeys were playing against the California Angels on September 15, 1990, Ken, Sr. showed what setting a good example for your son can do. In the first inning the senior Griffey stepped up to the plate with a man on first and promptly smashed a home run into the stands. Ken Griffey, Jr. was the next Seattle batter. Like a good son he got into the batter's box and followed his father's example. He too crashed a home run!

YOUNG SWINGER

Tony Conigliaro of the Boston Red Sox holds the major-league record for the most home runs by a teenager. Conigliaro blasted 24 round-trippers in 1964 when he was just 19 years old.

THE HARD CELL

Pitcher Lefty Gomez of the New York Yankees was a player who was always ready with a funny answer. Lefty was once scheduled to pitch an exhibition game for a team whose first baseman was having income-tax problems. Gomez was asked how he felt about having a first baseman who might be in jail when the game started. "Well," said Lefty, "it'll be an awful long throw for the shortstop."

HEADGEAR GOOF

Baseball fans in Spokane, Washington did a double take when a batter for the Albuquerque Dukes came to bat in a Pacific Coast League game in 1979. The batter, Bobby Mitchell, stepped up to the plate wearing a football helmet on his head! Mitchell wore the helmet to protect a cheekbone he'd fractured earlier in the season.

NOBODY'S PERFECT

In 1947 Ted Williams of the Boston Red Sox was almost a perfect player. He won baseball's Triple Crown by leading the American League in batting with a .343 average, runs batted in with 114, and home runs with 32. Unfortunately, Williams didn't steal a single base that year.

YOU AGAIN?

Relief pitcher Darold Knowles of the Oakland A's set a World Series record in 1973 by pitching in all seven games of the World Series against the New York Mets. Oakland won the series 4–3.

FREQUENT FOUR-SACKERS

Just how good was Babe Ruth at hitting home runs? Experts have figured out that Ruth hit a home run every 11.76 times he appeared at the plate! Second only to the Babe in home-run-hitting frequency is Harmon Killebrew of the Minnesota Twins, who whacked a round-tripper every 14.22 times he got up.

UNDERHANDED HURLER

Eddie Feigner was a famous softball pitcher whose fastball was clocked at 104 miles per hour. On February 8, 1967, he appeared with a celebrity softball team in a charity game against some of major-league baseball's greatest hitters. In that contest, Feigner struck out six major-league greats all destined to become members of baseball's Hall of Fame. The players were Willie Mays and Willie McCovey of the San Francisco Giants, Brooks Robinson of the Baltimore Orioles, Roberto Clemente and Maury Wills of the Pittsburgh Pirates, and Harmon Killebrew of the Minnesota Twins. And just to top things off, Eddie Feigner struck out all six of them in a row!

ZEROS EVERYWHERE

In 1972 super pitcher Nolan Ryan, then a member of the California Angels, set a record by shutting out eight different teams during the season.

HEY JOE!

It was hard to call a ball hit into the outfield against the Brooklyn Dodgers in 1940. If you yelled, "Joe's got it!" you were in trouble. That season Joe Medwick played left field, Joe Vosmik was in center, and Joe Gallagher played right field for the Dodgers.

NEATNESS COUNTS

Nippy Jones of the Milwaukee Braves wasn't the greatest major-league player, but he was one of the neatest. In the 1957 World Series against the New York Yankees, his neatness really counted. Pinch-hitting late in the game, Nippy told the home-plate umpire that a pitch had hit his foot. The Yankee catcher said that the ball had hit the ground. The ump hadn't seen the play and wasn't sure. Jones told the umpire to check the ball for a trace of polish, because he'd just polished his shoes before the game. Sure enough, the ball had polish on it! Jones was awarded first base, and that started a rally that helped the Braves win the contest!

WINNING WAYS

P itcher Bob Gibson of the St. Louis Cardinals was almost unstoppable in World Series play. Pitching for the Cards in the 1964, 1967, and 1968 World Series, Gibson set a record by winning seven straight games on the mound.

NO OUTS

P itchers Mike Palagyi of the Washington Senators and Jim Schelle of the Philadelphia Athletics both lasted only one year in the major leagues. Palagyi and Schelle both pitched during the 1939 season. One reason their big-league careers were so short is that neither one of them got a single batter out that season!

A LITTLE POWER

W ho says you have to be a big person to be a power hitter? Mel Ott of the old New York Giants, who hit over 500 home runs during his major-league career, was only five feet, nine inches tall. Sometimes big hitters come in small packages.

5' 9"—

511
HRs

POWERFUL PACK

I n 1950 the Boston Red Sox had a powerful hitting lineup. That season eight members of the Boston team ended up with season batting averages over .300. The Red Sox sluggers were Billy Goodman (.354), Dom DiMaggio (.328), Al Zarilla (.325), Walt Dropo (.322), Tom Wright (.318), Ted Williams (.317), Johnny Pesky (.312), and Birdie Tebbetts (.310). But hitting isn't everything, unfortunately. The Boston Red Sox finished third in their league that season.

ALL-STAR THIRD BASEMEN

T he 1967 baseball All-Star contest was a low-scoring game, and had to go 15 innings before the outcome was finally decided. The National League won the game by the score of 2–1. What made the contest so strange was that all three runs were scored on homers hit by All Stars playing the same position. Dick Allen and Tony Perez homered for the National League while Brooks Robinson smashed a round-tripper for the American League. Allen, Perez, and Robinson were all third basemen.

FAMILY FEUD

When the Chicago Cubs played the Philadelphia Phillies on September 20, 1986, the two teams' opposing pitchers were very familiar with each other. In fact, they grew up together. Pitching for Chicago was 20-year-old Greg Maddux. On the mound for Philadelphia was 25-year-old Mike Maddux, Greg's older brother. Unfortunately, when it comes to pitching, players don't have much brotherly love. Greg Maddux beat his older brother Mike by the score of 8–3.

JUST BE THOUGHTFUL

New York Yankee catcher Yogi Berra was a great hitter, but often swung at pitches out of the strike zone. Manager Casey Stengel tried to break Yogi of his bad habit. "Study the pitcher," Stengel said. "Study every throw carefully." Shortly after Stengel's speech, Berra went to bat and struck out on three perfect pitches. "What did you expect me to do?" Yogi growled when he returned to the bench. "Swing and think at the same time?"

GREAT ARM

Hugh Daly enjoyed a pretty good major-league career back in the 1880's. In one game he hurled a no-hitter. In another contest he struck out 16 batters— at a time when it took *four* strikes to get a man out. What made Daly's achievements so unusual was that he had only one arm!

WALK DON'T RUN

Pittsburgh Pirates TV announcer and former pitcher Jim Rooker completed the longest walk of his baseball career on October 18, 1989. The walk covered 337 miles and took 12 days to finish.

It all began when Rooker was broadcasting a Pirates-Phillies game on June 8, 1989 from Philadelphia. The Pirates quickly jumped out to a 10–0 lead over the Phillies. Rooker was certain Pittsburgh would win to end a six-game losing streak, so he said to TV fans, "If we lose this game, I'll walk home." The Pirates ended up losing 15–11. Rooker didn't walk home from Philadelphia to Pittsburgh that night, but his comment created such a stir that he promised to live up to his vow after the season ended, and indeed he did.

On October 5, 1989 Rooker began his long walk from Philadelphia to Pittsburgh, collecting donations for charity along the way. Finally, after 12 days of walking and lots of blisters, Jim Rooker finished his charity trek by reaching Pittsburgh. It just goes to prove that TV announcers have to watch what they say on the air!

TWICE THE HERO

I n the third game of the 1991 World Series, the Minnesota Twins and the Atlanta Braves were deadlocked 4–4. The game, which began on October 23, 1991, was still tied after midnight. So it was actually October 24 when Braves' outfielder Mark Lemke came to bat in the twelfth inning with team-mate David Justice on base. Lemke delivered a single to score Justice and win game three for the Braves 5–4.

The two teams met again for game four the evening of October 24. In that game, with the score tied 2–2 in the ninth, Lemke tripled and then scored the winning run on a sacrifice fly by Jerry Willard. So Atlanta infielder Mark Lemke ended up being a hero of two World Series games in a single day!

GOOD AND BAD

P itcher Phil Niekro of the Atlanta Braves had a good year and a bad year on the mound in 1979. Phil led the National League that season with 21 wins, but he also led the league with the most losses—20. Phil Niekro was the first pitcher in this century to lead the league in both wins and losses.

BASE BAMBOOZLED

Lloyd Moseby of the Toronto Blue Jays came up with a unique style of backward base-running in a game against the Chicago White Sox. It started with Moseby on first base. Lloyd tried to steal second, but didn't see a wild throw from the Chicago catcher go into the outfield. Moseby thought the batter hit a fly ball into the outfield. Not wanting to be doubled off of first base if the ball was caught, Moseby, who was safe at second, got up and ran back to first! The White Sox center fielder picked up the catcher's wild throw and fired to first to try to get Moseby out. But the throw from the outfield bounced by the first baseman. Moseby touched first and, seeing the ball go wild, turned around and dashed back to second again. For the second time Lloyd was called safe as he slid into second base!

THEY MEASURED UP

When a Kansas City Athletics pitcher served up a pitch to Dave Nicholson of the Chicago White Sox on May 6, 1964, the pitcher had no idea he was delivering a record-setting ball. Nicholson cracked the ball an amazing 573 feet for a home run. It was the longest measured home run in a regular-season major-league game.

LONG-TERM CONTRACT

Clarence "Red" Faber spent 20 years in the major leagues and pitched over 4,000 innings of baseball. Amazingly enough, Red did all of that while playing with the same team. Faber began and ended his long career with the Chicago White Sox.

BRAVE SLUGGERS

Only one team in major-league history has ever had three men on its roster each hit 40 or more home runs in a season. That team was the 1973 Atlanta Braves, and the hitters were Dave Johnson (43 home runs), Darryl Evans (41 home runs) and Hank Aaron (40 home runs).

WHAT A DAY!

Infielder Joe Torre couldn't do much right at the plate on July 21, 1975 while playing for the Mets. Torre hit into four double plays in one game to set a National League record.

QUICK START

Joe "Iron Man" McGinnity is best remembered as a tireless pitcher who could hurl inning after inning of winning baseball in the early 1900's. However, Joe was a quick starter, too. He won 27 games his first year in the major leagues pitching for the old Baltimore Orioles of the National League.

The next year he moved to the Brooklyn Dodgers, where he won five games in his first six days on the team. He also won 22 more games his first season with Brooklyn. Now that's a pretty good start to a major-league career.

SHORT STAY

Pitcher Bill Caudill, who played for the Seattle Mariners in 1982, was traded that year to the New York Yankees. But Bill wasn't on the team long enough to even try on a uniform. He spent only 20 minutes in the Yankee organization before being traded back to Seattle!

HIT MAN

Catcher Wilbert Robinson of the old Baltimore Orioles once got seven hits in seven trips to the plate. Wilbert cracked six singles and a double in a game on June 19, 1892, to set a major-league record that went unequaled for almost 80 years.

COPY CATS

In 1979 Ken and Bob Forsch combined to set an interesting major-league pitching record. Of course, being brothers who are both major-league pitchers is something out of the ordinary, but that wasn't enough for Ken and Bob. Bob Forsch of the St. Louis Cardinals started things off by pitching a no-hitter against the Philadelphia Phillies on April 16, 1978. Copycat Ken of the Houston Astros equaled his brother's feat a year later by no-hitting the Atlanta Braves on April 7, 1979. The Forsches are the first brothers in baseball history to both throw no-hitters.

A SMALL RECORD

Frank "Home Run" Baker led the American League in home runs four times during his career. However, his total number of homers for all four of those years was only 40 round-trippers! Baker led the AL with 9 home runs in 1911, 10 in 1912, 12 in 1913, and 9 in 1914!

NO ZEROS PLEASE!

The New York Yankees once played 308 consecutive baseball games without being shut out a single time. The record-setting Yankee streak ran from August 2, 1931 to August 3, 1933!

FOUL DEED

When Babe Ruth was a pitcher for the Boston Red Sox, he found Buck Weaver of the Chicago White Sox a tough player to pitch to. In one at-bat, Buck didn't blast a home run off the Babe, but he did foul off 17 consecutive pitches.

FAMOUS BUNCH

The 1932 New York Yankees had a lot of great players on their team. In fact, nine of the Yankee players on that squad were eventually voted into baseball's Hall of Fame. The distinguished members of that team were Babe Ruth, Lou Gehrig, Herb Pennock, Bill Dickey, Red Ruffing, Earle Combs, Lefty Gomez, Joe Sewell, and Tony Lazzeri. By the way, the manager of the 1932 Yankees, Joe McCarthy, was also voted into the Hall of Fame.

BIG WINNER

Talk about luck. Talented Gene Conley was a member of the Milwaukee Braves when they won the World Series in 1957. The following year he was a member of the Boston Celtics basketball team when they won the NBA championship in 1958!

BUT WHAT ABOUT BABE?

Babe Ruth, one of the greatest baseball players in the history of the game, set numerous records during his career, but was never voted the Most Valuable Player of the American League!

JINXED!

Pitcher Hub Pruett was never elected to the Hall of Fame, but he sure was a jinx to one of the Hall's most famous players. Pruett, who pitched for the St. Louis Browns, struck out slugger Babe Ruth 19 of the 31 times they faced each other.

MOUND MARK

Dutch Levsen of the Cleveland Indians was the last major-league hurler to pitch and win *both* games of a doubleheader. On August 28, 1926 Dutch hurled two 9-inning games back to back, winning 6–1 and 5–1.

MIRACLE MAN

If a pitcher is lucky enough to throw a no-hitter in his career, the odds are slim he'll ever pitch another one. But lefty Johnny Vander Meer accomplished an amazing feat in 1938. Vander Meer, who had a blazing fastball, was a member of the Cincinnati Reds that season. On June 11, 1938 Johnny excited the baseball world by hurling a no-hitter against the Boston Braves. Unbelievably, Vander Meer threw another no-hitter *in his very next outing,* on June 15, 1938 against the Brooklyn Dodgers! No other pitcher in history has ever thrown two consecutive no-hitters.

DESTINATION UNKNOWN

Babe Herman of the old Brooklyn Dodgers was an athlete, not a scholar. When Charles Ebbets, the owner of the Dodgers, offered Babe a trip around the world as a bonus, Herman replied, "Frankly, I'd prefer somewhere else!"

ARM TROUBLE

In 1907 Yankee catcher Branch Rickey had a tough day behind the plate. He set a major-league record by allowing runners to steal 13 bases in a single game!

BOARD GAME

One key to success for many businesspeople is to start small and then grow with the company. Apparently that holds true for the business of baseball. Young Bowie Kuhn once had a job operating the scoreboard at Washington's old Griffith Stadium. He later grew up to be the commissioner of Major League Baseball.

STREAKERS

Pitchers Rube Marquard of the old New York Giants and Tim Keefe of the New York Metropolitans share an amazing mound record. They both won 19 games in a row during their careers. In 1888 Keefe was the first to chalk up 19 straight wins. Marquard equaled Keefe's mark in 1912.

ONE GREAT DAY

John Paciorek was a great athlete who signed to play pro baseball with the Houston Colt 45's in 1963 at age 17. That year, he was brought up to the major leagues for Houston's final game of the season. John went 3 for 3, scored 4 runs, walked twice, and drove in 3 runs. After the 1963 season, Paciorek returned to the minors and never played major-league ball again. But John Paciorek sure had an outstanding one-game major-league career!

HEADED FOR HOME

Pitcher Pat Caraway of the Chicago White Sox pulled some wacky stunts during his major-league career. During his rookie year, Caraway, a native of Gordon, Texas, found the late-season weather in Chicago not much to his liking. One extremely cold and windy day Pat started complaining about the chilly weather and wouldn't stop. "What do you want me to do about it?" the Chicago manager finally said to his disgruntled pitcher.

"Well, can I at least go home and get an overcoat?" Pat asked.

"Sure," said the manager. "Go home and get it."

So wacky Pat Caraway left Chicago and went all the way home to Gordon, Texas to get his overcoat.

MOVE THE PLATE

Rex Barney was a hard-throwing pitcher for the Brooklyn Dodgers in the 1940's. Rex could fire bullets, but he had control problems—he walked more batters than he struck out. Sportswriter Bob Cooke once summed up Barney's career by saying, "Rex Barney would be the league's best pitcher—if the plate was high and outside."

OLD STORY

Carl Yastrzemski of the Boston Red Sox won the American League batting title in 1968 with a .301 average. It was the lowest average ever posted by an AL batting champion. When George Sisler, an old-time batting champ himself, was asked at the end of that season what he thought his average would be if he'd played ball in the American League in 1968, his answer was surprising. "Oh, I guess I would have done as well as Yastrzemski and hit about .300," Sisler said.

Since Sisler had compiled a lifetime average of .340 and hit over .400 twice during his career, some people were shocked by George's modesty. "Only .300?" one person asked.

"Don't forget," Sisler added jokingly. "At the time, I'd have been almost 75 years old."

KEEP TRYING

Babe Ruth, one of baseball's greatest home-run hitters, started his career as a pitcher and didn't really look like much of a slugger. In fact, Ruth hit only nine home runs during his first four years with the Boston Red Sox. Babe hit no homers in 1914, four in 1915, three in 1916, and two in 1917. Of course, after that, the rest is baseball history!

PASS THE MUSTARD

E d Glynn was a pitcher for the New York Mets during the 1980 season. But Glynn didn't make his first trip to Shea Stadium, the Mets' home field, in 1980. When Ed was a student at Francis Lewis High, a school in the area, he spent many hours at Shea— selling hot dogs. For that reason, the Mets honored him in May 1980 at a pre-game ceremony. What award was presented to Glynn at the ceremony? An official Shea Stadium hot dog, of course!

BIRD BRAIN

T he St. Louis Cardinals received a lot of negative press in 1978 when they lost their first six games of the season. So the team asked reporter Doug Grow of the *St. Louis Post-Dispatch* to write more positive stories about them in the paper. Grow agreed and shortly thereafter wrote, "The Cardinals only have 100 games remaining."

HUNG UP

Baseball player Arnie Moser really got hung up in the outfield one day while playing in the Southern League. Moser was in the outfield for his Nashville team when a player from the opposing Knoxville squad smashed a liner toward the scoreboard. Arnie raced toward the scoreboard and leaped high into the air to snare the ball, but missed! The ball hit the wall and bounced back onto the playing field. Moser hit the wall and stuck there, his belt snagged on a peg in the wooden fence! Arnie Moser ended up dangling in the air above the field. The other Nashville outfielders had to go over and help him down.

WHAT A DAY

August 4, 1985 was a big day in baseball history. On that day pitcher Tom Seaver got his 300th career win. Four hours later, at another game on the same day, slugger Rod Carew got his 3,000th hit!

HOME-RUN MACHINE

The great Babe Ruth once slammed 125 home runs— in one hour! Ruth put on his amazing hitting show before an exhibition game in February 1927. Six different pitchers threw at him for an hour as he slammed home runs out of the park at the rate of two per minute!

CLOSE SHAVE

When the Pittsburgh Pirates won the National League pennant in 1960, one of the happiest Pirates fans around was a man from Dubois, Pennsylvania. Clinching the pennant not only took a load off that  fellow's mind, but also one off his chin. Back in 1953, that loyal fan had sworn not to shave again until the Pirates won a pennant. True to his word, he stayed away from razors for seven long, hairy years. Finally, in 1960, the Pirates won the title and their loyal fan in Dubois got a shave!

I'M NOT OLD

Pitcher Phil Niekro of the New York Yankees notched his 300th victory on October 5, 1985 with an 8–0 win over the Toronto Blue Jays. But winning his 300th career game wasn't the only achievement Phil accomplished with that win. He also became the oldest pitcher in baseball history ever to record a shutout. Niekro was 46 years, 188 days old when he blanked the Blue Jays, thus eclipsing Satchel Paige in the baseball record books. Paige, of the St. Louis Browns, was 46 years, 75 days old when he shut out the Chicago White Sox on September 20, 1952.

TOUGH LUCK

Most players count themselves lucky just to be in the major leagues. But pitcher Dave Stieb of the Toronto Blue Jays had to be questioning his luck during the 1988 season. On September 21, 1988 Stieb had a no-hitter going with two outs in the ninth inning against the Cleveland Indians. Up stepped Julio Franco, who quickly spoiled Stieb's no-hitter by stroking a single. The very next game Stieb pitched, he had another no-hitter going in the ninth inning, this time against the Baltimore Orioles. But bad luck struck again. With two outs in the ninth, Jim Traber poked a single to ruin Stieb's no-hitter. Poor Dave Stieb. He had two consecutive no-hitters spoiled by hits with two outs in the final inning of both games!

DOCTORING UP THE BALL

Pitcher Bobby Brown, who played for the New York Yankees, was nicknamed Doc Brown for a good reason. Bobby Brown became a surgeon when his playing days ended.

SIGNING OFF

A sign on a ballpark in Kansas City in 1882 read: Please do not shoot the umpire. He is doing the best he can!

THAT'S A CROWD?

W hen the New York Mets took on the Pittsburgh Pirates at Shea Stadium on September 30, 1980, the result was a bit depressing for the Mets. First off, the Pirates won the game 3–2. If that wasn't bad enough, only 1,754 fans showed up to watch the teams in action. The low turnout left 53,546 of Shea's seats empty!

WHAT A CARD

B aseball-card collecting is a big hobby. One of the rarest baseball cards in the world is a 1933 Napoleon "Nap" Lajoie card. When the Goudy Gum Company issued their 1933 baseball-card series, they forgot to include one of second baseman Nap Lajoie, who retired from baseball in 1916. To fix their mistake, the card company issued the 1933 Nap Lajoie card in 1934. The future Hall of Famer's card soon became scarce. Only twelve 1933 Nap Lajoie cards are now known to exist.

TWO-DAY CELEBRATION

J ohn Cooney played mostly for the Brooklyn Dodgers and the Boston Braves during his 20-year baseball career. Cooney came to bat 3,372 times during his stay in the majors, but hit only two home runs. Amazingly, those home runs came on consecutive days—September 24 and 25, 1939.

FAST BALL

M ost people know that Nolan Ryan is one of the fastest pitchers in baseball history, and Ryan proved it in 1974. While a member of the California Angels, Ryan threw a pitch at Anaheim Stadium on August 20, 1974 that was clocked at 100.9 miles per hour!

WHAT'S THE SCORE?

P itcher Dave Rowe of the old Cleveland Spiders had a disastrous outing on July 24, 1881. On that day Rowe gave up 35 runs in a single game to set a major-league record.

FOLLOW THE BOUNCING BALL

You've heard that baseballs sometimes take strange bounces. But in the early days of baseball, a bouncing ball could get a batter into real trouble. Until 1864, a batted fair ball caught after one bounce was considered an out. And until 1883, if a batter hit a foul ball that was caught on one bounce, he was called out, too!

YOUNG DUDE

Lou Boudreau was only 24 years old when he was named manager of the Cleveland Indians in 1942.

ALMOST PERFECT

Tom Browning of the Cincinnati Reds had a perfect game going against the Philadelphia Phillies on July 4, 1989. Tom's perfection lasted until the ninth inning. With one out to go, the Phillies' Dickie Thon spoiled Browning's perfect game by hitting a double. The very next month Toronto Blue Jay hurler Dave Stieb suffered the same fate as Tom Browning. Stieb had a perfect game going with two outs in the ninth inning against the New York Yankees on August 4, 1989. Then up stepped Roberto Kelly, who drilled a double to ruin Stieb's bid for perfection.

DUEL ON THE MOUND

One of the greatest pitching duels in baseball history took place in a game between the Cincinnati Reds and the Chicago Cubs in 1917. Fred Toney was on the mound for Cincinnati. Jim "Hippo" Vaughn was the Chicago hurler. For nine innings, pitchers Toney and Vaughn held opposing batters hitless. They both had no-hitters going into the tenth inning of play. It was the only time in baseball history that two opposing pitchers both had no-hitters for nine innings. In the first extra inning Fred Toney kept his no-hitter alive by getting three fast outs. Unfortunately for Chicago, Jim Vaughn gave up a hit, and the Reds went on to score the game-winning run.

UNPOPULAR

In 1926 Sam Breadon, the owner of the St. Louis Cardinals, traded all-star Rogers Hornsby to the New York Giants for Frankie Frisch. St. Louis fans were so outraged that they actually hanged Breadon in effigy. The St. Louis Chamber of Commerce was so angry they denounced Breadon in a resolution. Many St. Louis fans never did forgive Sam Breadon for trading away their favorite star.

TWO SWINGS—EIGHT RUNS

Bob Allison and Harmon Killebrew gave their Minnesota Twins' club eight runs with two swings of the bat in 1962. That year Allison and Killebrew became the first players in baseball history to both hit grand-slam home runs *in the same inning!*

WHO STRUCK OUT?

S ammy White of the Boston Red Sox accomplished an unusual baseball feat on June 2, 1952. White struck out in a game while sitting on the bench. Here's how it happened: White was batting and took two perfect pitches for strikes without swinging. That made the Boston manager mad, so he yanked White out of the game and put in pinch hitter Bill Henry. Henry took a ball and fouled off a pitch before swinging and missing at strike three. Bill Henry was out. However, the rules of baseball state that whoever gets the first two strikes in an at-bat is charged with the out. Thus, Sammy White was officially charged with striking out even though he was on the bench.

ONE FOR YOU, AND ONE FOR YOU

Pitcher Cy Young was the first pitcher in baseball history to hurl no-hitters in both the National League and the American League. His National League no-hit performance came against Cincinnati on September 19, 1897, and his first American League no-hitter was against Philadelphia on May 5, 1904.

JUST DUCKY

The St. Louis Cardinals met the Detroit Tigers in the 1934 World Series, and it was a hard-fought contest. While playing in Detroit, Cardinal outfielder Joe "Ducky" Medwick hit a triple and slid hard into third base. Ducky's slide was so rough that he knocked over Detroit third baseman Marv Owen. Medwick and Owen got into a heated argument that almost resulted in a fight. When the inning ended, Medwick went to the outfield and was greeted by a chorus of boos from the Detroit fans. The angry fans even started to throw garbage, bottles, and other junk at Medwick from the stands. For his own safety Medwick had to be removed from the game. Ducky Medwick is the only player ever yanked from a World Series game for his own good.

DON'T PICK ON ME

Some baseball players chew gum or tobacco. Shortstop U.L. Washington of the Kansas City Royals had an odd habit. He always played with a toothpick in his mouth.

WHAT A DIFFERENCE A YEAR MAKES

Norm Cash of the Detroit Tigers won the American League batting crown with a .361 batting average in 1961. The following year Norm didn't do so well. His average dropped 118 points in 1962, to .243.

BIG-LEAGUE WELCOME!

Infielder Bert Campaneris was an instant hit in the big leagues in 1964. On July 23, 1964, Campaneris played in his very first major league game. In his very first at bat, he hit the first pitch thrown to him into the stands for a home run. Amazingly enough, nine other players have accomplished this strange feat in the history of major-league baseball.

WASHED-OUT RECORD

Everyone knows that Roger Maris broke Babe Ruth's home-run record of 60 round-trippers by hitting 61 homers in 1961. What most people don't know is that slugger Jimmy Foxx of the Philadelphia Athletics might have equaled Babe Ruth's mark in 1932 if Mother Nature hadn't turned against him.

In 1932 Jimmy Foxx belted 58 home runs to lead the American League. However, he also hit an additional two home runs that season that would have tied Ruth's record. Unfortunately for Foxx, he hit those homers in games that ended up being rained out—so the home runs didn't count!

DUCK DAVE!

All-Star outfielder Dave Parker spent some tough years in the outfield as a member of the Pittsburgh Pirates. In one game against the Montreal Expos in 1980, fans threw empty cans, apples, and chunks of ice at Parker as he stood in the outfield. But Dave kept his sense of humor. Commenting later on the incident he joked, "I wish they'd thrown barbecued ribs at me. I love barbecued ribs."

BAT MANIA

The first baseball-stadium bat day was held in 1952 at the St. Louis Browns' home stadium. The idea of the special day was the brain child of the Browns' Rudie Schaffer. After buying some 12,000 bats from a company that was going out of business, Schaffer decided to distribute free bats to fathers and sons who attended a doubleheader in June 1952. The idea caught on, and has been around ever since.

FOOD FOR THOUGHT

Bob Feller, the famous Cleveland Indians fireballer, joined Cleveland as a pitcher fresh out of high school. But before he became a member of the Indians, young Bob worked in the concession department at Cleveland Stadium.

NO REGULAR GUY

In 1964 the New York Mets just couldn't seem to find a third baseman they liked. Seven different players each played ten or more games at third base for the Mets that season. The players were Charley Smith, Ron Hunt, Bobby Klaus, Wayne Graham, Johnny Stephenson, Amado Samuel, and Rod Kanehl.

RUNS BATTED IN GALORE

Tony Cloninger of the Atlanta Braves was a busy man with the bat on July 3, 1966. Cloninger drove in nine runs in one game against the San Francisco Giants. Tony hit two grand-slam home runs and an RBI single in that contest. Believe it or not, that's not the record for most RBI's in a single game. James Bottomley of St. Louis set that record when he knocked in 12 runs in a game on September 16, 1924. And amazingly, Cloninger is not the only player to have hit two grand slams in a single game. *Seven* players share that record. What makes Cloninger's mark so unusual is that he was a *pitcher*, and pitchers aren't known for being the best hitters!

INDOORS, OUTDOORS

The Skydome is the home field of the Toronto Blue Jays of the American League. It has a retractable roof that can open when the weather is good or close when the weather is bad. On June 7, 1989, the dome was open when the Blue Jays took on the Milwaukee Brewers. But as the game continued, it began to rain, so the Skydome's roof was ordered closed. That's how a game that began outdoors was finished inside a closed stadium. It was the first indoor-outdoor game in baseball history.

THE OLD SWITCHEROO

In the early 1960's the Los Angeles Dodgers had an infield made up of Wes Parker, Jim Gilliam, Maury Wills, and Jim Lefebvre. What makes that interesting is that every member of that Dodger infield was a switch-hitter.

FIREBALLER

Walter Johnson was one of the hardest-throwing pitchers in the history of baseball, and he was also one of the most durable. Johnson pitched in a record 802 games during his career, winning 412 contests. He also pitched 113 shutouts. However, he only recorded one no-hitter during his 21-year baseball career.

BETTER WITH AGE

Ted Williams was the oldest player ever to win a batting title. The Boston Red Sox star was 40 years old when he won the title in 1958 with a .328 average.

GROUP WORK

O ne of the strangest no-hitters in baseball history occurred on September 28, 1975, in a game between the Oakland A's and the California Angels. Oakland pitcher Vida Blue held the Angels hitless for five innings. Blue was then replaced by Glenn Abbott, who continued to hold the Angels hitless for almost two innings. In came Paul Lindblad to pitch. He finished out the seventh inning and California remained hitless. Finally in stepped Rollie Fingers to pitch for the A's. No Angels got any hits off Fingers either. For the first time in history, four pitchers combined to hurl a no-hitter. Vida Blue earned the win, but Blue, Abbott, Lindblad, and Fingers all set the record. Amazingly, this record was matched by Bob Milacki, Mike Flanagan, Mark Williamson, and Gregg Olson of the Baltimore Orioles on July 13, 1991 when they combined to no-hit the Oakland A's.

WHAT A ROOKIE!

P itcher Grover Cleveland Alexander started his major-league career on a winning note. Alexander won a record 28 games on the mound in his very first season.

LEGAL SPITBALL

M ost baseball fans know that wetting a ball gives the pitcher an unfair advantage over the hitter. A wet ball can curve much more than a regular curve-ball. For that reason it is illegal to throw what is best known as a spitball. However, what many baseball fans don't know is that a spitball used to be perfectly legal in the major leagues. It wasn't until 1921 that throwing spitballs in baseball was banned.

ROUND-TRIPPER

Hall of Famer Josh Gibson of the Homestead Grays, a team in baseball's Negro Leagues, may have been the greatest home-run hitter of all time. Before black players were allowed on teams in the major leagues, Gibson reportedly hit 84 homers in one season, and 800 home runs in his career!

BUNNY BASEBALL

Walter James Vincent Maranville is a Hall of Famer most people recognize by his nickname of Rabbit! Rabbit Maranville was one of the smallest athletes ever to play in the majors. He was only 5 feet 5 inches tall and weighed 155 pounds. Despite his size, Rabbit was big on practical jokes. Once while his team was batting, he crawled through the legs of an umpire to get to the plate!

INDEX